Rochester History

FALL 2023

Rochester History

A publication of the Rochester Public Library
in partnership with Rochester Institute of Technology

Volume 81, Issue 1

Contents

In this edition of the *Rochester History* journal, Lisa Kleman examines a topic dear to many members of our community: music. The commitment of Rochesterians to the development of arts and culture in the early twentieth century is clearly conveyed in this recounting of conductor Hermann Dossenbach's year abroad, a trip financed by a cadre of residents eager to see the development of a professional orchestra and the elevation of local music. The dedication of the city's leaders to music is evident in the establishment of the Musical Council and in the financial support that allowed Dossenbach and his family to live in Berlin and experience firsthand the abundant and varied musical offerings of major European cities. Dossenbach's travels translated into a richer, more complex musical experience in Rochester. Any reader interested in how our city became a base for professional classical music will certainly learn new things from Kleman's article. ■

Patty Uttaro
Director, Rochester Public Library

LETTER FROM THE EDITORS

Dear reader,

In Rochester, George Eastman gets much of the credit for the community's educational and cultural richness. After all, the founder of the Eastman Kodak Company financed many—if not most—of the city's most well-known and enduring cultural institutions, including the Eastman School of Music, the Eastman Theatre, and the Rochester Philharmonic Orchestra. But one cannot fully understand Rochester's place on the musical map—both past and present—without also considering the musicians who shared their talents with the community. Though his name has largely been lost to history, Hermann Dossenbach was perhaps foremost among them. This issue of *Rochester History* explores just a small portion of Dossenbach's life: the year he spent in Europe in 1911–1912. Yet it reveals much about how and why the mid-sized city of Rochester could aspire to—and ultimately become home to—what is today a world-class orchestra and one of the nation's top music conservatories.

If you enjoy this issue, it is just the beginning. In early 2024, we hope to reveal the first digital edition of the journal. We are still working out some technical issues, so we do not yet have a launch date. The pilot issue will be an extension of this print issue. Online content will include a podcast featuring an interview with author Lisa Kleman, a Dossenbach descendent. She'll discuss her research and share anecdotes about how and why she began her (literal) journey to trace her ancestor's legacy. Readers will also have the opportunity to see pages from the diary, written by Dossenbach's daughter, that Kleman references in her article.

But let's not get ahead of ourselves. There's still more to be excited about in this print issue, as we debut a new feature. ROC Artifact explores history through a single artifact, document, or collection. For this issue, author Christopher Brennan highlights an East Rochester man's 1926 Ku Klux Klan membership certificate. The document, discovered in the East Rochester Historian's Office, demonstrates that the infamous KKK was active in Rochester and provided a clue that led to other evidence to elucidate the chapter's activities. We expect some readers will be surprised by what Brennan learned.

If you have objects that tell a story that you would like to see featured in ROC Artifact in the future, please let us know. ■

Christine L. Ridarsky and Rebecca Edwards
Editors

Daisy Dossenbach. *Courtesy of Alma Faroo.*

The Dossenbachs in the 1920s. Hermann with daughters Hazel, Elsa, and Alma at right. *Courtesy of Alma Faroo.*

Transforming Music in the Flower City: Hermann Dossenbach's Year in Europe, 1911–1912

by Lisa Kleman

On July 29, 1911, Hermann Dossenbach; his wife, Daisy; and their three daughters set sail on the *USS President Lincoln*, bound for Berlin, Germany. They planned to live in the city for the better part of a year, then travel throughout Europe and England before returning home to Rochester. Dossenbach was a locally famous musician and conductor, and his trip was being funded by wealthy civic-minded Rochesterians intent on improving the city's musical and cultural offerings. The endeavor marked part of a broader effort among local leaders in the 1910s to expand Rochester and make it a more dynamic and attractive city, a vision perhaps best captured in the 1911 publication *A City Plan for Rochester*, the pages of which boasted majestic drawings of city halls, civic centers, and a library, as well as impressive reimaginings of Rochester's parks, streets, bridges, railroads, and canal beds.[1]

The previous year, the Rochester Chamber of Commerce had chosen the slogans "Do It for Rochester" and "Rochester Made Means Quality" in a bid to enhance the city's standing. Rochester Oratorio Chorus Director George Barlow Penny recoined the first phrase as "Do It for Musical Rochester" for his 1910 program, *The Creation*. The slogan was used for other musical events

Lisa Kleman retired from teaching English at Assumption College and Worcester State University in Massachusetts in 2013 and moved to Rochester to research and write about her ancestors, the Dossenbachs. She has conducted research at the archives of the George Eastman Museum, the Rochester Public Library, the Sibley Library, and more. In 2014, Kleman spent one year at GEM reading all of Eastman's letters; she also served as the program director for the Eastman Museum Council for two years.

"Do it for Rochester!"—one of two city mottos the Chamber of Commerce launched in 1910. From The Rochester Chamber of Commerce Twenty-Second Annual Dinner program, March 18, 1910, at Convention Hall. *From Hermann Dossenbach Papers A.D72, Rare Books, Special Collections, and Preservation, River Campus Libraries, University of Rochester.*

"Rochester Made Means Quality." From The Rochester Chamber of Commerce Twenty-Second Annual Dinner program, March 18, 1910, at Convention Hall. *From Hermann Dossenbach Papers A.D72, Rare Books, Special Collections, and Preservation, River Campus Libraries, University of Rochester.*

thereafter.[2] Such civic boosters and cultural connoisseurs aligned forces in the 1911–1912 movement to create a Musical Council, which envisioned the future Rochester as home to a widely renowned orchestra that would support and attract the most regarded performers of the age. Hermann Dossenbach's trip to Europe would serve as both the enterprise's maiden voyage and something of an intelligence-gathering mission, whereby the conductor would observe and absorb all the lessons his overseas counterparts had to offer and then bring them back home to Rochester. Such efforts, aimed at transforming Rochester into a center of culture, predated the creation of the Eastman Theatre and School of Music by a decade, but one can see the philosophical underpinnings of the Eastman enterprises in the early twentieth-century hopes, dreams, and ideas of many of Rochester's citizens, including Dossenbach.

The Musical Dossenbachs

Hermann Dossenbach came from a musical family. His father, Matthias, had been forced to emigrate from Baden, Germany, following the revolutions of 1848–1849 and arrived in the United States in 1851. He had a difficult time earning a living but was well-versed in the violin, so he taught lessons to supplement his meager income as a comb-maker. In fact, the entire family played together, according to an old friend who knew the Dossenbachs when they lived in Suspension Bridge Village in Niagara Falls, New York. "I was about eight years old when I used to trudge up to his [Matthias's] house at night to take lessons on the violin," recalled E.C. Theilig. "Mrs. Dossenbach played the Bass viol, her sister the Cello, and two daughters played first, and the little boy (about six years old) and I tried to play second. The lad was so small he had trouble holding his violin while playing."[3]

Matthias Dossenbach, circa the 1870s. *From Rochester Photographic Files D.309, Rare Books, Special Collections, and Preservation, River Campus Libraries, University of Rochester.*

Like the Dossenbachs, many of Rochester's immigrant families enjoyed playing music together. In 1817, when Rochester was still in its infancy, English émigré Joseph Perkins, Sr., played with the very first local music group and was named bandleader of the Rochester City Band. His Canadian-born son, Joseph Perkins, Jr., eventually replaced him and founded several groups that performed for canal boats and various celebrations. His son, Joseph Perkins III, carried on the legacy, eventually becoming president of the Rochester Musicians Protection League.[4] Another prominent musical family in Rochester, the Schencks, included father Henry and his sons, Emil and Ludwig. Emil performed with Dr. Leopold Damrosch's New York Symphony Society in the early 1880s, while Ludwig taught many Rochester musicians, including violinist David Hochstein, and formed the Rochester Symphony Orchestra, an amateur but much-lauded local ensemble.

Henri Appy, a renowned violinist and conductor from Holland settled in Rochester in the mid-1800s and formed the Rochester Philharmonic Society (circa 1865–1866). He often performed with his brother, Ernest, and son, Henri, Jr.[5] In fact, it was Appy who, upon "discovering" Hermann Dossenbach's brother Otto in 1872, convinced the Dossenbachs to move to Rochester from Suspension Bridge Village.[6] Appy gave Otto and his three brothers, Adolph, Hermann, and Theodore, lessons and opportunities to perform with the Rochester Philharmonic Society. Otto, the "little boy" in the aforementioned letter and the eldest of the brothers, became successful as a child prodigy and was known as Rochester's "Wonderful Boy Violinist" throughout the 1870s and 1880s.[7] The next oldest Dossenbach, Adolph, was also a violinist. He occasionally joined Otto in performances and later

A circa 1885 portrait of Hermann Dossenbach's violin teacher, Henri Appy. *From the Collection of the Rochester Public Library's Local History & Genealogy Division.*

Hermann Dossenbach (at left) with J. G. Averell, circa 1890–1893, in Emily Sibley Watson's garden on Prince Street. *Courtesy of Rare Books, Special Collections, and Preservation, River Campus Libraries, University of Rochester.*

served as the director of both the Genesee Falls Band in the late 1890s and the Lyceum Theatre from approximately 1896 to 1910.

Hermann Dossenbach, born in 1868, once recounted that though his father made him take violin lessons, his interest wasn't piqued until he saw the Theodore Thomas Orchestra.[8] Thomas, often credited with shaping the role of symphonies in American cities, toured the country for decades, beginning in 1869 with his own orchestra and later as director of the New York Philharmonic and Chicago Symphony orchestras. Thomas popularized the works of Richard Wagner in the United States and was responsible for debuting many composers—including Bruckner, Dvorak, Elgar, Glazunov, Grieg, Massenet, Smetana, Tchaikovsky, and Richard Strauss—on American soil.[9] When young Hermann witnessed Thomas in action, he realized then and there that he wanted to become a conductor. From that moment forward, he worked diligently and exhibited a relentless focus.

Dossenbach Quintette plus harpist at George Eastman's retreat in Oak Lodge, North Carolina, circa 1908. Top Row (L to R): J. B. Paddon, Hermann Dossenbach, Theodore Dossenbach; at bottom: George Henricus, Arthur Metzdorf, and an unidentified harpist. *From Rochester Photographic Files D.309, Rare Books, Special Collections, and Preservation, River Campus Libraries, University of Rochester.*

Hermann Dossenbach's Rise to Rochester Prominence

In the late 1880s and early 1890s, Hermann Dossenbach performed both as a solo violinist and with his newly organized quartet at local events for influential, wealthy people who would become his patrons; among them were James Wadsworth, Emily Sibley Watson, and George Eastman. In the late 1880s, Hermann formed the Dossenbach Orchestra, initially as a society orchestra providing music for social events throughout Rochester and in surrounding towns.[10] Such ensembles differed from symphony orchestras in that they played engagements funded by specific patrons or organizations rather than formal concerts funded by ticket sales. Rochester, like many American cities, boasted a number of society orchestras and singing groups at the turn of the twentieth century, such as Meyering's and Moll's orchestras, the Tuesday Musicale, and the Festival Chorus. Dossenbach's success in this realm was undoubtedly influenced by the fact that he was both a tireless worker and quite charming. His daughter Hazel remembered him as a "social lion."[11] One of Dossenbach's longtime patrons was George Eastman, founder of the Eastman Kodak Company, who first hired the Dossenbach Quartette in 1905 to perform twice-weekly musicales from September through May at his East Avenue mansion. He also engaged the Dossenbach Orchestra to play for the occasional party. The Dossenbach Quartette—often a quintette when Hermann's youngest brother Theodore joined them, playing the standup bass—would entertain Eastman's guests for the next fourteen years.

Though they continued to perform at society functions in the early twentieth century, Dossenbach's outfit became a symphony orchestra in 1900 when it performed a formal concert in the lavish Mirror Room of the Powers Building. Dossenbach had achieved his dream, but there was still much work to be done. He developed the ensemble into a viable and much-lauded mid-sized city orchestra

Hermann Dossenbach's Contemporaries

Rev. Clarence Barbour Dossenbach's good friend and bowling partner. President of the Rochester Theological Seminary in 1915 and of Brown University in 1928.

William Barry Son of Patrick Barry of Ellwanger & Barry Nursery. In 1911, he was chairman of the Highland Park Committee.

Edgar N. Curtice Of Curtice Brothers Co., producers of canned and preserved food products. In 1910, Curtice purchased a season's subscription to the Dossenbach Orchestra for eight seats.

James G. Cutler Architect, inventor of the Cutler mail chute, and mayor of Rochester from 1904 to 1907. He wrote to Dossenbach in 1904, expressing how much he loved the Dossenbach Orchestra's concerts.

Edwine Danforth An early supporter of the Dossenbach Orchestra and the wife of lawyer Henry G. Danforth. Danforth sat next to Emily Sibley Watson and architect Claude Bragdon during concerts from 1908 to 1910. In 1927, Dossenbach and the Rochester Park Band gave a concert on the Danforth property at 200 West Avenue.

Theodore Dossenbach Hermann's brother and founder of the Rochester Park Band, which he directed until his death in 1924. Hermann took over as director until his own death in 1946.

George Eastman Founder of Eastman Kodak Company, major philanthropist, and patron of the Dossenbachs. The Dossenbach Quintette regularly played at his East Avenue mansion.

James E. Furlong Concert promoter.

Jeremiah G. Hickey Cofounder of Hickey-Freeman Co., clothing manufacturer.

Walter Hubbell George Eastman's attorney and Dossenbach's acquaintance. The Dossenbach Quintette occasionally performed at the Hubbell residence instead of at the Eastman mansion when Eastman was out of town.

over the course of the decade, but by 1911, he had become discouraged.[12] Eastman and other wealthy Rochesterians backed him through patronage, but it was never enough to properly support the orchestra. While Dossenbach had been able to continually expand his ensemble and choose more ambitious works, he still couldn't always perform the music he preferred. Though the pieces that the thirty-member orchestra played were positively reviewed, they were largely considered to be "light music," rather than serious works.[13]

Since Dossenbach's orchestra wasn't based in a big city, he wasn't able to attract players of certain instruments that would allow for a greater repertoire.

Laura Kimball Active in local charitable activities and arts organizations, she was married to the founder of the Kimball Tobacco Co. and was the sister of sculptor J. Guernsey Mitchell.

Dr. Montgomery Leary Former coroner's physician for the west side of Monroe County and public health expert who often worked with Dr. George Goler. In 1911, he became the first superintendent of Iola Sanitarium.

J. Redfern Mason Music critic who often wrote the program notes for the Dossenbach Orchestra.

Francis B. Mitchell President of the Post-Express Printing Company—publishers of the *Post Express* newspaper—and music director at St. Peter's Presbyterian Church.

Mary Mulligan A good friend of George Eastman along with her husband, Dr. E.W. Mulligan, who was Eastman's physician. The Dossenbach Quintette occasionally performed at the Mulligan home instead of at the Eastman mansion when Eastman was out of town.

Rush Rhees President of the University of Rochester from 1900 to 1935.

Ludwig Schenck Founder and conductor of the Rochester Symphony Orchestra.

William A. Searle Rochester journalist from 1906 to 1914 and active in local dramatic associations.

Hiram W. Sibley Son of Western Union founder Hiram Sibley. In 1904, he established the Sibley Music Library.

Jimmy Wadsworth Member of the influential Wadsworth family of Geneseo. In the 1890s, Dossenbach played for their annual hunts.

Emily Sibley Watson Philanthropist and daughter of Western Union founder Hiram Sibley. Watson was a good friend to Dossenbach and sponsor of his musical endeavors.

He regularly hired musicians from New York City for specific concerts, but that meant he couldn't have as many rehearsals as needed, since they didn't live in the area and his budget was limited. All of these concerns, and more, were on Hermann's shoulders alone.[14] To appearances, being an orchestra leader was a grand affair, so most of Dossenbach's music-going public would not have been aware of the struggles he faced. His friends and peers often noted that he invested more money into his orchestra than he made from it. University of Rochester President Rush Rhees informed the Ad Club convention in October 1912, "There is not a man in Rochester, a man more wholly devoted to doing a thing without regard to any financial return than Hermann Dossenbach has been in regard to his orchestra. For twelve years that man has given the best of his energies and thought without receiving a penny of compensation. Many have thought because the orchestra was known as the Dossenbach Orchestra that there was a splendid 'rake off' for Hermann, but the only 'rake off' he got was what he took out of his own pocket to pay off deficiencies."[15] Eastman occasionally paid for the ensemble's deficits, as he also did for Ludwig Schenck's Rochester Symphony Orchestra, which shared members of Dossenbach's ensemble, but such piecemeal support would not be able to sustain a symphony orchestra in the long run.

Rush Rhees and the New Musical Council

Dossenbach's ambitions would be buoyed by the rising tide of civic boosterism that swept the country in the 1910s. One of the ways this movement manifested itself in Rochester was through a growing interest in building up the city's cultural offerings. At the time, Europe was still considered the center for classical music. Americans still looked overseas for direction, and all great classical musicians in the United States were "European-authorized," with pedigrees from the great European teachers. Though Herman Dossenbach had received his violin instruction from his German father, Matthias, and the respected Hague-born Appy, who had played with Jenny Lind and was once court violinist for the King of Holland, his entire musical education had taken place in Rochester.[16] To keep pace with growing expectations and to help enhance Rochester's cultural standing, Dossenbach would need stronger European affiliations.

To accomplish this goal, local music critic J. Redfern Mason proposed creating a musical council in Rochester and sending Dossenbach to Europe. In January 1911, George Eastman informed Mason that he approved of the idea.[17] By May, the council had been established.[18] The group consisted of

George Eastman, circa 1911. *Courtesy of George Eastman Museum.*

Rush Rhees pictured in the 1912 University of Rochester yearbook. *From* Interpres, *1912, LD4747.I62, Rare Books, Special Collections, and Preservation, River Campus Libraries, University of Rochester.*

representatives from the city's major musical organizations (including the Dossenbach Orchestra, Tuesday Musicale, Symphony Orchestra, Oratorio Society, and Musicians' Union); music critics from daily newspapers; musically inclined members of the general public; the mayor; and the presidents of the Board of Education, the Chamber of Commerce, and the University of Rochester. Rush Rhees, representing the university, invited Eastman to join as a member of the public grouping alongside other wealthy and culturally minded citizens, such as William Barry, Edwina L. Danforth, J. E. Furlong, J. G. Hickey, Mary D. Mulligan, Hiram W. Sibley, and Emily Sibley Watson. Eastman, however, informed Rhees that he did not have the time to serve on the Musical Council.[19] Rhees nevertheless kept him apprised of pertinent matters, and, in turn, passed Eastman's wishes and opinions on to the council, as is evidenced in Rhees's correspondence. He admitted in a letter to Dossenbach that he always discussed orchestra matters with Eastman first.[20]

In June 1911, Eastman informed Rhees that he wished to pay up for his part of "Dossenbach's European matter," which amounted to $1,350 of the $4,500 total.[21] Further correspondence between the two that month detailed Rhees's increasing involvement in city musical matters, evinced by his collaboration with the recent May Festival and his growing appreciation of Dossenbach and his orchestra. In his June letter, Rhees credited Dossenbach with "the demonstration of a power, self-possession, and competency on the part of the orchestra that no one supposed they had acquired."[22] Rhees also informed Eastman that May Festival guest soloist Madame Bernice de Pasquali's manager, who had experience with the great orchestras of the day, had described the Dossenbach Orchestra as "an institution of far more than city-wide significance." The manager commented to *The Post Express* that he "thought Dossenbach a remarkable leader, to have been able to develope [*sic*] such an orchestra." The newspaper agreed, writing, "Mr. Dossenbach's industry is tireless, his enthusiasm infectious, his disregard of mere personal aggrandizement an example of artistic idealism to command respect and affection."[23]

Convinced of Dossenbach's talents and potential, the Musical Council began following through on Mason's proposal that Dossenbach and his family spend a year in Germany, where the musician would go to concerts, study conductors, and improve his violin techniques under the tutelage of a great European teacher so that he could "realize all the possibilities that are in him." The council felt that if Dossenbach took in all the available European musical trends and brought his accrued knowledge, inspiration, and ideas back home, it would "enable him to raise Rochester higher in the musical plane than it has yet stood."[24] The trip would be funded by a group of eminent Rochesterians, including Eastman, Rhees, Laura M. Kimball, Mary D. Mulligan, Hiram W. Sibley, and Emily Sibley Watson. And so it happened that from August 1911 to August 1912, Hermann Dossenbach and his wife, Daisy (both 43 years old), and their daughters, Hazel (19), Elsa (15), and Alma (12), lived in Berlin and traveled throughout Europe and England. The details of the family's glittering, musical year are vividly documented in Dossenbach's many newspaper interviews, scrapbooks, letters, and photos, as well as in Elsa's daily diary.

Hermann's Wanderjahr in Germany

Dossenbach's impending departure was commemorated in newspaper articles and farewell celebrations. On July 17, 1911, members of the Dossenbach Orchestra and the Rochester Park Band (founded in 1904 by Hermann's brother Theodore and directed by him until his death in 1924) held a banquet for the conductor at the popular Teall's Hall on East Avenue. Speakers included Mason,

Walter Hubbell, the Rev. Clarence Barbour, Dr. Montgomery Leary, and Ludwig Schenck. Six days later, the Lake Avenue Baptist Church, where Dossenbach's Quintette had been playing every Sunday, hosted a "Dossenbach Day."[25] On July 26, the Dossenbachs left Rochester's New York Central train station. They met Hermann's older brother, Adolph, in New York City, where they stayed at the Grand Union Hotel. They enjoyed the sights of the city—walking over the Brooklyn Bridge, riding up Riverside Drive, visiting Bronx Park, and taking the elevated train to Battery Park. There they saw the aquarium and "watched immigrants land," as Elsa noted in her diary. They also visited the newly built New York Public Library, which had opened to the public two months prior. They had lunch at Macy's, shopped at Wanamaker's and Huyler's—a chocolate and candy company—and ate dinner at a German restaurant, "just to get used to it you know," Elsa commented.[26]

On July 29, the family sailed out of Hoboken, New Jersey, on the *USS President Lincoln*. A week later, they landed at Plymouth, England, then sailed to Cherbourg, France, passing by Dover and gazing at the Chalk Cliffs before arriving in Germany, first at Cuxhaven, then Hamburg, and, finally, Berlin on August 11. The five Dossenbachs stayed in temporary

The New York Central and Hudson River Railroad Depot in Rochester. *From the collection of the Rochester Public Library's Local History & Genealogy Division.*

An early twentieth-century postcard of the Brooklyn Bridge. *From The DS Collection, the Postcard Archive at Florida State University.*

An early twentieth-century postcard of the New York City Public Library. *From The Miriam and Ira D. Wallach Division of Art, Prints and Photographs: Picture Collection, The New York Public Library. New York Public Library Digital Collections.*

Hermann Dossenbach (seated at center) onboard the USS Lincoln with unidentified friends. *From Rochester Photographic Files D.309, Rare Books, Special Collections, and Preservation, River Campus Libraries, University of Rochester.*

lodging before moving into their apartment on September 1. Elsa's diary provides the best record of the family's early experiences in Germany. Elsa and her siblings studied German and planned to enroll in school. Elsa took music lessons, which she found challenging, and explored Berlin, at first always chaperoned by a family member or a close family friend. She was thrilled by the Automat, a cafeteria-style restaurant in which diners selected their meals from vending machines, describing it as a "spiff place."

Almost immediately, the family began a constant round of going to musical performances, with Hermann and Daisy often including their two older daughters, Hazel and Elsa. On September 9, Dossenbach wrote Eastman that the family was getting settled into their four-room apartment. The orchestra season didn't start until October 9, but the opera season was already underway, and he had seen seven operas the previous week. According to Elsa's diary, these performances included *Samson and Delilah, Aida, Salome, Die Meistersinger,* and *Hansel and Gretel.* Dossenbach informed Eastman that he had arranged for violin lessons from a Professor van Laar, who taught at Henri Marteau's Hochschule für Musik in Berlin.[27] In their first month in Germany, the Dossenbachs also heard a performance by cellist Paulo Gruppe prior to his winter tour of the United States. They invited Gruppe, who had been born in Rochester but lived in the Netherlands from 1897 to 1913, to dinner two nights later. Elsa reported that his presence at dinner was quite a shock: "On the stage he looks so mild and meek and then to have such a deep voice he ought to be ashamed. He is very entertaining and can talk a blue streak."

Dossenbach's violin instructor, Willy Hess. *From Hermann Dossenbach Papers A.D72, Rare Books, Special Collections, and Preservation, River Campus Libraries, University of Rochester.*

In early October, the family saw Josef Stransky conduct the Blüthner Orchestra before he left Germany to direct the New York Philharmonic. Additional highlights that month included performances by Julia Culp, the Gelose Quartet at the Beethoven Saal, and the young American violinist Eddy Brown, who played eight encores until the house turned out the lights and started to lock the doors. The Dossenbachs regularly saw the Popular Concerts and the Berlin Philharmonic under Hungarian conductor Arthur Nikisch, sometimes with sandwiches in their pockets, and sometimes following the performance with a visit to a restaurant to get Bratwurst and beer.[28] Elsa was thrilled when her mother would give her and Daisy a "little sip of bier." In November, Hermann, Daisy, and Elsa heard Willy Hess perform. Hess had recently been concertmaster for the Boston Symphony Orchestra and was teaching violin at Berlin's Royal Academy of Music. Elsa was delighted to meet him at a Nikisch concert that December. Hess soon became Hermann's violin instructor in Berlin. Before the close of the year, Hermann, Daisy, and Elsa heard the twenty-year-old violinist Mischa Elman, who was "perfectly wonderful." Elsa described how the "crowd stayed until they turned the lights out" while Elman played four encores.

over to dinner Thursday.

Wednesday 27. After dinner mother & Hazel went downtown. Hazel got a hat and its really good looking but you have to look at it a while to get used to it. We didn't know that today was my birthday until mother happened to discover it was the 27 when she was reading the newspaper. She gave me a perfectly dear enamel locket. I got a letter from Lois and a postal from Mrs Leary. In the evening papa & I went to a concert given by the graduating class of Georg Bertram. They were all <u>awfully</u> good but the last one was too good to be true. Mother & Hazel went to hear a chorus of 140 singers. They said it wasn't as good but there was a piano player who was very good. Sweet sixteen and — — —

Thursday 28. After school Hazel and I went downtown and got some flowers. Paul Gruppe came over to dinner. It was quite a schock.

Hermann Dossenbach's fifteen-year-old daughter Elsa dutifully kept a diary of the family's year abroad. The main topics of interest featured in the journal are those one might deem typical of a teenage girl—clothing, friends, boys, and fun activities such as the thrill of occasionally being allowed to drink some beer—but her writings also provide a unique glimpse into the rich world of classical music in which the Dossenbachs were ensconced. The following excerpts detail Elsa's observations of life in Berlin, October 27–30, 1911.

over to dinner Thursday.

Wednesday 27. After dinner Mother & Hazel went downtown. Hazel got a hat and it's really good looking but you have to look at it a while to get used to it. We didn't know that today was my birthday until mother happened to discover it was the 27 when she was reading the newspaper. She gave me a perfectly dear enamel locket.
I got a letter from Lois and a postal from Mrs. Leary [Mrs. Montgomery Leary].
In the evening papa & I went to a concert given by the graduating class of Georg Bertram. They were all awfully good but the last one was too good to be true. Mother & Hazel went to hear a chorus of 140 singers. They said it wasn't so good but there was a piano player who was very good. Sweet sixteen and ___ ___ ___.

Thursday 28. After school Hazel and I went downtown and got some flowers.
Paul Gruppe came over to dinner. It was quite a schock [*sic*].

on the stage he looks so mild
and meek and then to have
such a deep voice he ought to be
ashamed. He's very entertaining
can talk a blue streak.
We went to hear some songs
and a symphony by Siegmund
and there was never such
a farce as that.
Friday 29. Went to my music
lesson. She didn't think much
of the concert by Bertram's pupils.
Mother and Hazel came home
from a walk and mother
had on the most peculiar
hat I've seen in a long time
One of those high affairs with a
wing on each side. She changed
the wings and now it looks good
Saturday 30 Went to school. The
French teacher and the English
teacher were raising the dickens
Fräulein Clepine was there but
she didn't seem to mind it.
In the afternoon mother and I

On the stage he looks so mild and meek and then to have such a deep voice he ought to be ashamed. He is very entertaining can talk a blue streak. We went to hear some songs and a symphony by Siegmund and there was never such a farce as that.

Friday 29. Went to my music lesson. She didn't think much of the concert by Bertram's pupils. Mother and Hazel came home from a walk and mother had on the most peculiar hat I've seen in a long time. One of those high affairs with a wing on each side. She changed the wings and now it looks good.

Saturday 30. Went to school. The French teacher and the English teacher were raising the dickens. Fräulein Clepine was there but she didn't seem to mind it. In the afternoon mother and I . . .

The Dossenbachs took great advantage of the educational and cultural opportunities available to them in Germany but otherwise led a relatively middle-class existence while overseas. Though they were being supported financially, they weren't flush with money. They went shopping but bought conservatively; Elsa and her mother chose Elsa's winter clothes in August but waited to buy them until a later time. In December, they finally purchased a pin she had been wanting for quite some time. Elsa's diary reveals that the Dossenbachs were a close-knit family. She made little mention of family strife—save for a minor reference to a "disagreement" with "Mama" on September 9—and often described the family partaking in activities together. Her diary is filled with mentions of "Hazel, Mama and I" or "Papa, Mama, and I" or "Hazel, Alma and I."

The family was kept apprised of the day-to-day goings-on in Rochester by letters from friends back home. In December, the Dossenbachs received letters from good friends Clarence and Florence Barbour and Walter and Adelaide Hubbell, who sent $10 in Christmas money to each of the three daughters, causing Elsa to comment, "My but I feel rich." They also heard from the Leach family. Monty, as Dossenbach called Montgomery Leach, wrote that he had ruptured his appendix in November. This nearly killed him, and he spent three weeks recovering in Dr. Lee's Private Hospital on Lake Avenue. Stating that Dr. Lee said he pulled through the burst appendix because he "was not loaded with tobacco and whiskey," Leach advised his friend to "take this as a warning and cut them both out."[29]

The local Rochester newspapers were occasionally updated on Dossenbach's activities in Berlin, sometimes by Rhees, who in February 1912 advised Hermann to write to him or Walter Hubbell "quite frequently . . . telling as much as you will about the concerts you have heard and the work that you are doing . . . in order that we may keep something going in the papers rather constantly."[30] Rochesterians learned that Dossenbach had rejoiced in hearing pieces by Beethoven, Brahms (including his C Minor quartet), Max Bruch, and Saint Saëns; piano concertos by D'Albert, Tchaikovsky, and Rubinstein; and a performance by the Cesar Franck Piano quintet. One local paper reported in the fall of 1911: "Of the new men, Mahler has vastly impressed him, especially the C Minor Symphony," which Dossenbach had just heard for the third time. When asked about the experience of hearing the hour-and-a-half-long symphony, he quipped: "It was not a minute too long."[31] As Dossenbach took pleasure in these impressive performances, he also studied their conductors intently. "Nikisch is a most wonderful man," he exclaimed in a circa 1911 interview, " . . . the moment he appears on the stage you can feel his presence and, from the first note of the orchestra, you realize that a master is at the helm and you settle down to enjoy his readings, confident that nothing can go wrong."[32] Interestingly, Nikisch, a leading interpreter of Wagner, was known for conducting without any scores in front of him. He was principal conductor of the Berlin Philharmonic when Dossenbach saw him but was on the verge of taking the London Symphony Orchestra on tour to the United States the following April.[33]

Arthur Nikisch, ca. 1920–1925. *From the George Grantham Bain Collection. Library of Congress, Prints & Photographs Division, LC-DIG-ggbain-32770.*

When Dossenbach wrote to Eastman following the latter's visit to Germany in February 1912, he provided a summary of his concert-going—discussing specific composers, conductors, and concerts. Foremost was Nikisch, whom he described as "one of the world's greatest conductors."[34] He also stated that he would see the last Richard Strauss concert at the Royal Opera House in April, adding excitedly: "By the way I heard 2000 Children [*sic*] sing German Folk Songs at Circus Busch. It was one of the most inspiring concerts I have ever heard."[35] He later described seeing another impressive performance, the "festival to Mahler, in which one thousand persons took part in the Eighth Symphony, a wonderful performance."[36] Witnessing these musical extravaganzas was having a noted effect on Dossenbach, for in early 1912, he wrote Rhees that he was interested in appointing a large chorus so that his orchestra could present Beethoven's Ninth Symphony. Rhees cautioned him to take on this enterprise at a later time, as "it would be wiser to get the orchestra well started before going after the choral situation with too much aggressiveness."[37]

That spring, Rhees started laying the groundwork for the orchestra Dossenbach would lead upon his return. In April, the university president wrote to Eastman to invite him to a planning session for the upcoming orchestra season at the Genesee Valley Club and reported that:

> Mr. Dossenbach has been at work in Berlin with utmost industry and enthusiasm since September last and he will return to Rochester in August, equipped to do better work for the musical interests of the city

> than he has ever done. It is but just to him to remark that his labor of twelve years for the development of his orchestra has been wholly a labor of love—at times even a source of actual expense to him. He has a rare spirit as well as high ability.[38]

The meeting established an orchestra committee, which engaged the Lyceum Theatre for a series of six concerts with the aim of showcasing "a soloist of worldwide fame" for at least three of these performances. The committee further concluded that: (1) orchestra members should be paid more so that Dossenbach could command more rehearsals, (2) Dossenbach should be given just compensation, and (3) the name of the orchestra should be changed to avoid public association with the former society orchestra.[39] The total expense would be $15,000, one-third of which would come from ticket sales; the rest would need to be underwritten. In August 1912, Eastman agreed to put forth $2,000, thereby becoming the orchestra's principal underwriter.[40]

In May 1912, Dossenbach updated his most generous patron, reporting that attending "217 concerts in 217 Days besides my studies have made it a very busy winter for me and I am looking forward to my work at home."[41] In return, Eastman shared news about the Dossenbach Quartette/Quintette, which he had continued to hire in Hermann's absence for twice-weekly musicales at his East Avenue mansion. The ensemble was temporarily led by concertmaster and first violinist James Paddon. When Paddon contracted diphtheria that month, Hermann's brother Theodore, who generally played the stand-up bass, substituted on the first violin. Eastman recounted that "the way he sailed in and pulled off the job was amazing."[42]

Before the family left Europe in July 1912, Dossenbach obtained a testimonial and recommendation regarding his excellent violin work from his instructor, Willy Hess, and penned a final letter to Eastman describing the last leg of his Wanderjahr: "After leaving Berlin 'June 3' we went to Dresden, Nuremberg, Rotenburg, Munich, Lucerne, Mayence, Bonn, Köhn, Brussels, Hague, Schweringen, Amsterdam, and London. I have been very fortunate in hearing a great deal of good music on the trip . . . in almost every city we visited." He continued, "Here in London the Royal Opera Co alternates with the Russian Ballet and are to continue until the end of the month so I am practically living at the Covent Garden Opera House." Dossenbach ended the letter by conveying his immense gratitude to Eastman: "Words cannot express how deeply I am indebted to you for making this trip possible."[43]

Hermann Dossenbach's Return and His Influence in Rochester

On July 27, 1912, the Dossenbach family departed Europe, and after a ten-day trip across the ocean, they reached New York City. At the landing dock, the Dossenbachs met up with their friends the Barbours and the Learys, who were just arriving from a vacation in Bermuda. The family returned to Rochester a few days later. As one local paper noted, "However much Mr. Dossenbach may have enjoyed his tour . . . he does not hesitate to say that Rochester looks better to him just now than any place he has seen. . . . 'When I once started for home, I couldn't get here quick enough.'"[44] Dossenbach's return was widely covered in the local newspapers. The *Democrat & Chronicle* boasted: "There is not a composition of major class that will be on any of this year's programs that Mr. Dossenbach did not study under the most favorable circumstances. He heard them directed by Strauss, by Nikisch, by Hausegger, the three greatest names in European music on the orchestra side, not once, but several times."[45]

Rochesterians learned of the many inspiring performances that the Dossenbachs witnessed overseas, including the four Wagnerian operas, "Der Ring des Nibelungen" (in Dresden), a students' torch parade in the university town of Heidelberg, several concerts by the Lamoureux Orchestra in the Dutch watering resort of Scheveningen, and a performance of the famous Oberammergau Passion Play put on by Hungarian peasants.[46] Such reports undoubtedly inspired some local readers to question what was preventing their own city from hosting such a culturally rich calendar of events. Dossenbach, for one, felt that the classical music standards to which European countries held themselves could indeed be replicated in America. While in Berlin, he had heard what he referred to as the three master organizations in Europe—the Königliche Kapelle, or Royal Orchestra, at the Royal Opera House, under the direction of Richard Strauss; Nikisch's Philharmonic Orchestra; and the Blüthner Orchestra, directed by Sigmund Hausegger. He nevertheless maintained that they weren't any better than the Boston Symphony Orchestra, Walter Damrosch's New York Symphony Orchestra, or Thomas's Chicago Orchestra. The *Democrat & Chronicle* reported that after hearing many of the great orchestras of Europe, Mr. Dossenbach "is of the opinion that American Orchestras measure fully up to their standard."[47] Charged with the task of directing a viable American orchestra, Dossenbach remained bullish on the possibilities of American music, even as he was mindful of the challenges he might face in implementing this vision in a mid-sized American city.

Hermann Dossenbach's Rochester Orchestra in Convention Hall, ca. 1912. *From the collection of the Rochester Public Library's Local History & Genealogy Division.*

In October 1912, a few months after Dossenbach's return, the season for the newly rebranded Rochester Orchestra was announced in the newspapers. The impressive orchestra committee, under Dossenbach's leadership, was comprised of Rush Rhees, chairman; Walter S. Hubbell, secretary; Mary D. Mulligan, treasurer; and William A. Searle, assistant secretary. It also included George Eastman, Emily Sibley Watson, Hiram W. Sibley, Francis B. Mitchell, James G. Cutler, and Edgar N. Curtice. The committee excitedly announced a line-up of eminent soloists for the first season: Madame Frances Alda, soprano; Efrem Zimbalist, violinist; M. Edmond Clement, tenor; David Bispham, baritone; and Rochester's own John Adams Warner, pianist. Madame Carmen Melis, soprano, was added at a later date.

The influence of Dossenbach's European tutelage became clear at a Sunday Musicale at Eastman's house on October 27, after which Hubbell wrote Dossenbach: "I never heard you play a solo with such feeling and power and purity of tone as you did the Beethoven number.... If you can do for the orchestra what you have done for yourself, you are bound to have a big winter and a bigger future."[48] The impact on his conducting was apparent at the Rochester Orchestra's first concert at the Lyceum Theatre in November. "From the moment when Mr. Dossenbach walked out upon the stage and lifted his baton," one reviewer wrote, "there was evident that intangible and elusive feeling of confidence in both conductor and orchestra." The reviewer further described the sensation of "justifiable pride and well-being" that people there felt "in helping Rochester's musical and artistic appreciation to keep pace with its civic and commercial progress."[49] All reviews described the concert as a great success and an exciting sign of things to come.

While Rochester experienced a period of civic and commercial progress in the 1910s, Dossenbach contributed to the city's cultural progress. As he transplanted to American soil the lessons, compositions, ideas, and concepts he absorbed in Europe, Dossenbach planted the seeds for a major transformation in Rochester's music scene. He worked tirelessly over the course of the decade, in his bid to put Rochester on the musical map, to develop the Rochester Orchestra into a reputable ensemble. His efforts were not in vain. Each concert season surpassed the previous one. The music the orchestra selected and performed grew more impressive each year, and attendance numbers steadily increased (though they were never as high as hoped—this is the way it goes with orchestras). As a further testament to Dossenbach's efforts, the greatest of the world-renowned classical stars began including Rochester on their tours. In addition to the aforementioned soloists, guests in the 1910s included violinists Fritz Kreisler, Carl Flesch, Eddy Brown, and Tosca Seidel; pianists Ossip Gabrilowitsch (also guest conductor), Josef Hofmann, and Leopold Gadowsky; sopranos Madame Julia Culp, Madame Johanna Gadski, Madame Alma Gluck, Mabel Garrison, and Anna Case; baritones Putnam Griswold, David Bispham, Edmund Burke, Emilio De Gogorza, and Reinald Werrenrath; contraltos Margaret Keyes and Margarete Matzenauer; tenors M. Edmond Clement, Walter Vaughan, and Giovanni Martinelli; and basso Clarence Whitehall.

Dossenbach Introduces the European Model to Rochester

Dossenbach's European experience had convinced him that it was possible for a mid-sized city to sustain and support such a high-caliber orchestra. He informed the *Democrat & Chronicle* in 1912, "no German city of more than 30,000 inhabitants is without its permanent symphony organization, while few American cities of less than 250,000 population have high-grade symphony organizations."[50] As he shared his European observations with local newspapers in the years following his trip, he helped reimagine what could be done in an American city such as Rochester. He noted the low price point of popular concerts in Berlin and the fact that concerts were well attended and given frequently, such that holding and going to concerts became part of

Program from the Rochester Shakespeare Pageant of 1916. *From Hermann Dossenbach Papers A.D72, Rare Books, Special Collections, and Preservation, River Campus Libraries, University of Rochester.*

the general expectations of public life. Even though Dossenbach would never have the resources to conduct Beethoven's Ninth, his time in Europe had heightened his aspirations and inspired him to take on increasingly impressive musical feats. The Shakespeare Pageant of 1916 showcased both Dossenbach's ambition and the European pricing model. The event marked an early example of the kind of grand-scale production that Dossenbach hoped would find a welcome home in Rochester. The massive spectacle featured 2,500 characters, a chorus of 1,000 voices, and an 80-piece band and orchestra under the leadership of the Dossenbach brothers—with Hermann as orchestra director and Theodore as band director. Seeking to broaden his potential audience, Dossenbach made 2,000 free seats available at each performance in addition to the tiers of paid tickets.

Two additional trends that Dossenbach had observed in Europe in the early 1910s were implemented in Rochester the following decade. A local reporter noted that "one of the things that struck [Dossenbach] forcibly is that the [European] orchestras are often engaged by ambitious composers to try out their new works. When it is remembered what difficulty young composers in this country sometime have in getting a hearing, the advantage of this arrangement becomes obvious."[51] This kind of enterprise would later become a hallmark of Howard Hanson's reign at the Eastman School of Music. The director actively sought to showcase and promote new American talent, launching his American Composers Orchestral Concerts in 1925.[52] The school's founders may have drawn direct inspiration from Dossenbach's experience in Belgium as they planned one particular feature of the school. Dossenbach recounted to the *Lake Avenue Baptist Record* in 1912, "In Brussels I saw one thing that seemed to me excellent from an educational standpoint . . . there was an orchestra of thirty pieces on the stage, above them the screen for moving pictures and alternately the music and the pictures were given. The music was in part classic, in part lighter music, but it was all good music and the pictures were of a fine class."[53] Over the course of the 1910s, both Hermann, with his own orchestra, and his brother Theodore, with the Rochester Park Band, grappled with the musical balance of serious versus light music and the need to sell tickets. Before the end of the decade, Eastman had developed the plan to pair popular movies with live classical music—with the dual aim of educating the general populace about classical music and increasing the potential audience for what would become the Rochester Philharmonic Orchestra.

Dossenbach mused in 1912, "I think the reason the German appreciation of music is so great [is] because there are so many opportunities to hear good music that it becomes familiar just as the popular music does here, but I have every faith in our musical future."[54] He argued that the German people were passionate about classical music because they had been educated in regard to it: "The time will come when Americans will be educated to the same appreciation of music. We are making headway all the time and nowhere more than right here in Rochester. Give the people the best of things in music and they will come to like it and demand it."[55]

A Key Legacy

During the same decade in which Hermann Dossenbach helped Rochester reach new musical heights, he also cofounded the predecessor of the institution that would establish the city as an internationally renowned center of classical music. In 1913, one year after his return from Europe, Dossenbach and Swedish pianist Alf Klingenberg opened a music school, The Dossenbach-Klingenberg School. It was, of course, supported by George Eastman. In 1918, Eastman purchased the school—after it had been renamed the Institute of Musical Art and Dossenbach was no longer involved—for the University of Rochester. It was rebranded the Eastman School of Music in 1921.

Many former members of the Rochester Orchestra, which disbanded in 1919, along with other local performers and renowned European musicians who had flocked to the United States during and after World War I, would join the new Rochester Philharmonic Orchestra, which debuted in 1923. Sadly, Hermann Dossenbach would not be among them. Eastman had asked Dossenbach to conduct the Movie Theatre Orchestra, and though he initially accepted the offer, he changed his mind a few months later. A number of things may have influenced his decision. He may have been disappointed that he hadn't been asked to become the conductor of the Rochester Philharmonic Orchestra. Or he might have been turned off by the fact that he would have had to work under a younger, inexperienced musical director. It is also possible that he was daunted by the competition of the post-war influx of European musicians. However, above all these possibilities, it is more likely that a full understanding of the rigors of a silent movie orchestra—learning scores on the fly, not having enough time for preparation and rehearsal, giving repetitious performances—is what caused Dossenbach to pass on the offer. He nevertheless remained a committed participant in Rochester's music scene. Dossenbach would eventually perform at the Eastman Theatre in the capacity of guest conductor of the Rochester Civic Orchestra in 1933, but the main focus of his latter-day career would be the Rochester Park Band, which he took over in 1924 following Theodore's death. He continued directing the ensemble until his own death in 1946.

Epilogue

University of Rochester President Rush Rhees said of Dossenbach that Rochester "had a man and artist of whom it might well be proud."[56] An industrious optimist, Dossenbach strove to elevate Rochester's cultural offerings and, in turn, uplift his city. Much like the civic boosters who helped fund his Wanderjahr, he had every faith in Rochester's potential. As one local journalist insightfully opined in 1912: "Cities are known, not alone for their commercial ratings nor for the totals of their bank clearances, but also for their aspirations and pursuit of things of the spirit. . . . The first quarter of the twentieth century still has bound up in it the visions of those who dream that Rochester shall be found in the goodly company of cities which reach beyond gold to better things for those within their borders."[57] Hermann Dossenbach's aspirations were well-supported in the early twentieth century, and Rochesterians would receive the benefit of this support for years to come. ■

Acknowledgments

Most special were the friendships Kleman made with other Dossenbach ancestors—Lynn Charles, Alma Faroo, Jacqueline and Gary Fraser, and Polly Smith, as well as Annabelle Martin, who remembered Hermann Dossenbach from childhood visits, and Ruth Krautwurst Sorensen, whose uncle performed with Hermann and Theodore Dossenbach and who preserved a valuable historical collection that Kleman was thrilled to assist in donating to Sibley Music Library and the German-American Musicians of Buffalo.

Kleman is most grateful for the friendship, guidance, and research assistance from Vincent Lenti, Eastman School Historian and Professor of Piano—Vince kept Dossenbach's name alive via his historical writings for *Rochester History*, his fascinating presentations, and his book, *For the Enrichment of Community Life: George Eastman and the Founding of the Eastman School of Music*, as well as through Elizabeth Brayer, a dear friend and the author of *George Eastman: A Biography*. Kleman worked for Betsy in 2017 as a research assistant and then prepared Betsy's archives for donation to the George Eastman Museum and the University of Rochester's RBSCP.

1. Arnold W. Brunner, Frederick Law Olmsted, and Bion J. Arnold, *A City Plan for Rochester: A Report Prepared for the Rochester Civic Improvement Committee* (New York: Cheltenham Press, 1911).
2. George Barlow Penny, Program, *The Creation* (May 5, 1910).
3. E.C. Theilig to Hermann Dossenbach, April 20, 1922, Box 1, Folder 1.7, Correspondence, 1915–1929, Hermann Dossenbach papers, A.D72, Rare Books, Special Collections, and Preservation, River Campus Libraries, University of Rochester.
4. "Brief Profiles: Joseph H. Perkins, Jr. 1822–1882, musician," Rochester Historical Society.
5. "The Appys in Concert," *Democrat & Chronicle*, June 23, 1894.
6. "The Boy Violinist," *Buffalo Morning Express and Illustrated Buffalo Express*, March 7, 1874, quoted from the *Rochester Express*, March 28, 1873.
7. "Otto Dossenbach, The Wonderful Boy Violinist," advertisement, *Syracuse Daily Courier*, April 25, 1874.
8. Thomas played in Rochester frequently. It is likely that Dossenbach saw him for the first time in the late 1870s.
9. Charles Edward Russell, *The American Orchestra and Theodore Thomas* (New York: Doubleday, 1927).
10. Dossenbach was performing as a violinist as early as 1885. The Dossenbach Orchestra's earliest engagement appears to have been a circa 1887 concert for the Henry George Social Club at Kolb's Hall.
11. Hazel Dossenbach, interview by Vincent Lenti, February 7 and 12, 1980, private collection.
12. "A Civic Opportunity," *The Post Express*, November 16, 1912, in Hermann Dossenbach Scrapbook, vol. 3, Local History & Genealogy Division, Central Library of Rochester & Monroe County.

13. "Delightful Musical Event," *The Post Express*, February 6, 1900. Light music is considered a less-sophisticated form of western classical music, typically comprising shorter pieces designed for popular appeal.
14. "Encouragement for Dossenbach," *Democrat & Chronicle*, September 3, 1912.
15. "Pays Tribute to Dossenbach: Dr. Rhees Remarks on What Orchestra Man Has Done," ca. October 11, 1912, Hermann Dossenbach Scrapbook, vol. 3 Local History & Genealogy Division, Central Library of Rochester & Monroe County.
16. "Henri Appy," *Democrat & Chronicle*, November 17, 1903.
17. "Orchestra Leader to Go Abroad," July 18, 1911, Hermann Dossenbach Scrapbook, vol. 2, Local History & Genealogy Division, Central Library of Rochester & Monroe County; Letter, George Eastman to J. Redfern Mason, January 30, 1911, Book 7, Eastman Legacy Collection, George Eastman Museum.
18. Rush Rhees to George Eastman, May 2, 1911, Box 32, Eastman Legacy Collection, George Eastman Museum.
19. George Eastman to Rush Rhees, May 27, 1911, Book 7, Eastman Legacy Collection.
20. Rush Rhees to Hermann Dossenbach, February 14, 1912, Box 1, Folder 1.6, Correspondence 1912–1914, Hermann Dossenbach papers, A.D72, Rare Books, Special Collections and Preservation, River Campus Libraries, University of Rochester.
21. George Eastman to Rush Rhees, June 15, 1911, and July 5, 1911, Book 7, Eastman Legacy Collection.
22. Rush Rhees to George Eastman, ca. June 1911, Box 32, Eastman Legacy Collection, George Eastman Museum.
23. "In Musical Circles," *The Post Express*, July 1911, Hermann Dossenbach Scrapbook, vol. 2, Local History & Genealogy Division, Central Library of Rochester & Monroe County.
24. "In Musical Circles," *The Post Express*, July 1911, Hermann Dossenbach Scrapbook, vol. 2.
25. Dossenbach Day program, July 12, 1911, W. S. Hubbell Scrapbook, vol. 3, Box 3, Walter Sage Hubbell papers, A.H87, Rare Books, Special Collections, and Preservation, River Campus Libraries, University of Rochester.
26. Elsa Dossenbach, Diary, July 27, 1911, in the author's possession, courtesy of Alma Faroo (daughter of Elsa). Details of the Dossenbachs' doings in Berlin are taken from this diary and from cited newspaper articles and letters.
27. Hermann Dossenbach to George Eastman, September 9, 1911, Box 33, Eastman Legacy Collection.
28. The Popular Concerts of the Berlin Philharmonic Orchestra, especially in the pre-WWI era, were cheaper concerts that drew substantial audiences.
29. Montgomery Leach to Hermann Dossenbach, December 20, 1911, Box 1, Folder 1.5, Correspondence 1912–1914, Hermann Dossenbach papers.
30. Rush Rhees to Hermann Dossenbach, February 14, 1912, Hermann Dossenbach papers, Box 1, Folder 1.6, Correspondence 1912–1914, Hermann Dossenbach papers.
31. "Hermann Dossenbach, who is doing eight hours study each day . . ." newspaper clipping, ca. fall 1911, Hermann Dossenbach Scrapbook, vol. 2.
32. "Hermann Dossenbach, who is doing eight hours study . . ." newspaper clipping, ca. fall 1911, Hermann Dossenbach Scrapbook, vol. 2.
33. "Music: Nikisch and the London Symphony Orchestra," *The Nation*, April 18, 1912, Box 2, Folder 2.3, Clippings 1906–1920, Hermann Dossenbach papers.
34. Hermann Dossenbach to George Eastman, February 3, 1912, Box 34, Eastman Legacy Collection.
35. Hermann Dossenbach to George Eastman, March 28, 1912, Box 35, Eastman Legacy Collection.
36. "Mr. Hermann Dossenbach," September 1912, *Lake Avenue Baptist Record*, vol. 2, no. 11, Box 3, Folder 3.7, Miscellaneous Memorabilia, Hermann Dossenbach papers.

37. Rush Rhees to Hermann Dossenbach, February 14, 1912, Hermann Dossenbach papers, Box 1, Folder 1.6, Correspondence 1912–1914.
38. Rush Rhees and Walter Hubbell to George Eastman, April 6, 1912, Box 35, Eastman Legacy Collection.
39. Walter Hubbell to George Eastman, July 23, 1912, Box 36, Eastman Legacy Collection.
40. Walter Hubbell to George Eastman, August 8, 1912, Box 36, Eastman Legacy Collection.
41. Hermann Dossenbach to George Eastman, May 10, 1912, Box 35, Eastman Legacy Collection.
42. George Eastman to Hermann Dossenbach, May 4, 1912, Box 1, Folder 1.6, Correspondence 1912–1914, Hermann Dossenbach papers.
43. Hermann Dossenbach to George Eastman, July 6, 1912, Box 36, Eastman Legacy Collection.
44. "Hermann Dossenbach is again ready for Musical Season," ca. August 1912, Hermann Dossenbach Scrapbook, vol. 3, Local History & Genealogy Division, Central Library of Rochester & Monroe County.
45. "Dossenbach is Well Equipped," *Democrat & Chronicle*, October 27, 1912.
46. "Mr. Hermann Dossenbach," September 1912, *Lake Avenue Baptist Record*, vol. 2, no. 11, Box 3, Folder 3.7, Miscellaneous Memorabilia, Dossenbach papers, A.D72 Rare Books, Special Collections, and Preservation, River Campus Libraries, University of Rochester.
47. "Returns From Year in Europe with Masters," *Democrat & Chronicle*, August 8, 1912.
48. Walter Hubbell to Hermann Dossenbach, October 29, 1912, Box 1, Folder 1.6, Correspondence 1912–1914, Hermann Dossenbach papers.
49. "Lyceum Theater," November 18, 1912, Hermann Dossenbach Scrapbook, vol. 3.
50. "Returns From Year in Europe with Masters," *Democrat & Chronicle*, August 8, 1912.
51. "Hermann Dossenbach, who is doing eight hours study . . .," ca. fall 1911, Hermann Dossenbach Scrapbook, vol. 2.
52. Vincent A. Lenti, *Serving a Great and Noble Art: Howard Hanson and the Eastman School of Music* (Rochester, NY: Meliora Press, 2009), 66.
53. "Mr. Hermann Dossenbach," September 1912, *Lake Avenue Baptist Record*, vol. 2, no. 11, Box 3, Folder 3.7, Miscellaneous Memorabilia, Dossenbach papers, A.D72, Rare Books, Special Collections, and Preservation, River Campus Libraries, University of Rochester.
54. "In Musical Circles," *The Post Express*, August 10, 1912, Hermann Dossenbach Scrapbook, vol. 3.
55. "Hermann Dossenbach is again ready for Musical Season," ca. August 1912, Hermann Dossenbach Scrapbook, vol. 3.
56. "Pays Tribute to Dossenbach: Dr. Rhees Remarks on Orchestra Man," ca. October 11, 1912, Dossenbach Scrapbook, vol. 3.
57. "A Civic Opportunity," *The Post Express*, November 16, 1912, Dossenbach Scrapbook, vol. 3.

BOOK REVIEW

Declaring Disaster: Buffalo's Blizzard of '77 and the Creation of FEMA

by Timothy W. Kneeland. Syracuse, NY: Syracuse University Press, 2021.

Christine Keiner, Rochester Institute of Technology

After moving to Western New York in the early 2000s, I first realized the political gravity of winter weather when chatting with an RIT student who was serving in the National Guard. When I asked if his unit might have to deploy soon to Iraq or Afghanistan, he said, "No, we need to stay here to deal with the snow!"

Political historian Timothy Kneeland explains the origins of this situation in his illuminating book *Declaring Disaster*. While focusing on Buffalo, his analysis of the intertwined technological and political dimensions of devastating winter storms sheds light on the understudied Great Lakes Snowbelt, a region encompassing several cities, including Milwaukee, Chicago, Cleveland, Rochester, Syracuse, Boston, and Philadelphia. The narrative unfolds over three distinct eras: the early twentieth century, when the dismantling of streetcar systems necessitated new approaches to municipal mobility; the 1977 Buffalo blizzard and its complex causes and effects; and the event's long-term ramifications on managing lake-effect snowstorms.

The book opens with a fascinating discussion of what STS (science and technology studies) scholars would call the social construction of urban snowstorm disasters. Kneeland explains how the government officials who enacted policies prioritizing private cars over public mass

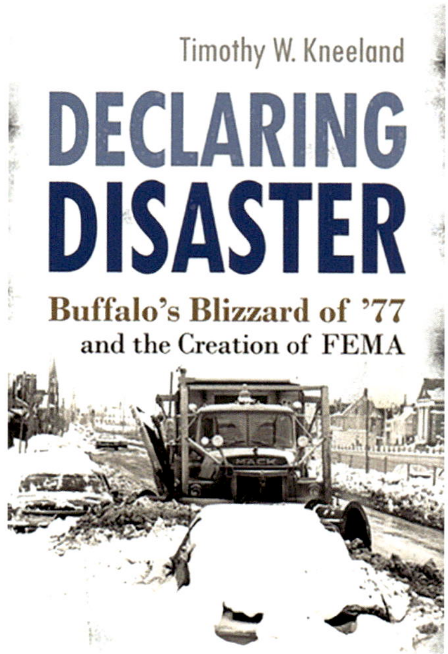

transit during the early-to-mid 1900s created the conditions for catastrophe during snowy and icy weather. When urbanites had to walk just a short distance or take a trolley ride to get to work and hospitals, shop for food, and obtain other needed goods and services, it was relatively easy to adapt to snowy surroundings. Pedestrians could change their footwear to brave the elements, and streetcar companies could hire workers or install plows to clear the tracks.

But all that changed by midcentury.

Timothy W. Kneeland. *From the author.*

Like other cities across the United States, Buffalo redirected public-transit funds toward massive highway systems designed to convey cars, buses, and trucks over long distances between urban centers and their far-flung suburbs. To keep traffic flowing over such dispersed areas in inclement winter weather, public-works officials adopted the "bare-pavement policy." Local governments assumed responsibility for removing all snow and ice on roads down to the dry pavement, a practice necessitating the purchase and maintenance of snowplow fleets as well as huge quantities of road salt—a corrosive, costly, and toxic deicing agent.

As Kneeland persuasively argues, automobility intensified the potential negative impact of winter storms in the Buffalo metropolitan region, and the bare-pavement program for rubber-tired vehicles "created conditions that were ripe for the disaster that occurred in 1977."[1] Moreover, as he shows by building upon the works of other urban- and disaster-studies scholars and by drawing upon previously unused archival documents, these changes were never inevitable; they evolved over decades as a result of deliberate decisions by government officials, corporate stakeholders, and powerful lobbyists such as the Salt Institute.

The greatest disaster in Buffalo's history began on Friday, January 28, 1977, when a blizzard struck at around 11 a.m. Buffalo had been experiencing one of its coldest winters, which had caused snow to accumulate on frozen Lake Erie, and, during the blizzard, gale-force winds generated sudden whiteouts that obliterated drivers' vision and stranded tens of thousands of people downtown and in the airport. The blizzard ultimately killed twenty-nine people, disrupted vital services for days, and cost hundreds of millions of dollars.

Because officials had already spent their entire snow-removal budget for the season—a function of deindustrialization and the city's declining tax base—Buffalo's mayor struggled to cope with the walls of snow and bad publicity.

Although he secured some local, state, and federal assistance for clearing roadways, Mayor Stanley Makowski later succumbed to pressure to withdraw his candidacy for reelection, ending his political career. Other elected officials at higher levels scrambled to demonstrate their responsiveness to their constituents by traveling to Buffalo and by convincing President Jimmy Carter to issue the nation's first major disaster declaration due to snow. As Kneeland describes, "politics permeated decision-making related to the blizzard."[2]

As conveyed in the subtitle, Kneeland also addresses the Buffalo blizzard as a turning point in US disaster policy. President Carter, who had just assumed office the week before the storm, resisted internal pressure to avoid setting a precedent by declaring Buffalo a disaster area and thus eligible for federal funds for snow removal. He worked throughout his tenure to reorganize the existing emergency management system by establishing a new entity, the Federal Emergency Management Agency (FEMA), led by a director responsible to the president.

Mindful of the political misfortunes of Makowski and other mayors who mishandled blizzards, elected leaders in the Snowbelt have worked hard since the 1970s to avoid becoming "the poster child for snow failure."[3] By cultivating better public relations with the media, issuing precautionary driving moratoriums, and investing in state-of-the-art forecasting, plowing, and anti-icing technologies, local and state authorities have reduced vulnerability to winter hazards. However, snow removal remains extremely expensive, and travel bans can backfire if announced too late or if conditions improve unexpectedly.

In his concluding chapters, Kneeland interprets the recent willingness of governors to impose driving bans in advance of snowstorms as a rejection of "the hegemonic control that cars have had in defining mobility for Americans."[4] He also cites public concern over the environmental effects of road salt, increasing support for public transportation systems that run on tracks, the rise of remote work and online shopping, a reduction in vehicle miles driven, and other factors as evidence of a "post-automobility era" during which Snowbelt winters may become less dangerous.[5]

At the same time, as he acknowledges, global climate change is posing new wintery threats to cities outside the traditional Snowbelt. While it will likely be a long time before Western New York and the United States implement systems that enable the majority of urban and suburban residents to live and work without cars, this book demonstrates the vital importance of avoiding the mistakes of earlier urban planners who failed to consider the unintended consequences of automobility. ■

1. Timothy W. Kneeland, *Declaring Disaster: Buffalo's Blizzard of '77 and the Creation of FEMA* (Syracuse, NY: Syracuse University Press, 2021), 10.
2. Kneeland, 71.
3. Kneeland, 103.
4. Kneeland, 126.
5. Kneeland, 132.

A Secret Revealed: Charles Ott and the Ku Klux Klan

Christopher Brennan, Librarian, Central Library of Rochester & Monroe County

The problem with secret societies is that they are, well, secret! Unless one belongs, it is hard to know who the members are or what their activities entail. This is especially true of a group with a racist reputation like the Ku Klux Klan. It is rare, therefore, when one discovers a local artifact that specifically identifies a member.

Among surviving Klan artifacts is a certificate dated November 1, 1926, naming Charles Ott as "Knight Kamellia," the first stage beyond probationary membership in the Ku Klux Klan.[1] We do not know exactly when Ott joined the Klan, but Klan regulations stipulated that a probationary member could be raised to the status of Knight Kamellia after six months,[2] which suggests he joined on or before May 1, 1926. The promotion likely was a reward for Ott's hosting the September 25–26, 1926, regional gathering of the Klan, which will be discussed later in more detail.

The Ku Klux Klan was formed after the Civil War to resist Federal efforts to remake the South and to defy the empowerment of formerly enslaved African Americans. During the presidency of Ulysses S. Grant (1869–1877), the Klan was suppressed, but the discriminatory values it harbored lived on long after. The Klan was revived following the success of *The Birth of a Nation*, a 1915 motion picture that glorified the Klan.[3]

The Klan entered Western New York in the early 1920s. Locally, an organizational meeting was held December 11, 1922, at the Knights of Malta Hall, 89 East Main Street, Rochester.[4] Another membership rally was held one year later, on November 22, 1923, in the original Reynolds Arcade building. A reporter who attended the latter event heard an organizer rant against Roman Catholics and Jews.[5]

The dates of the organizing efforts and the groups disparaged suggest why the Klan found some local followers. In November 1922, Alfred E. Smith was reelected governor of New York. Smith had been elected for the first time in 1918, lost his bid for reelection in 1920, but succeeded in the following election cycle. Born in New York City, the son of Irish immigrants, Smith found his strongest support among urban groups, particularly Roman Catholics, Jews, and newly arrived immigrants.[6] Nativist Americans, who feared the growing influence of those of foreign birth, responded positively to the Klan's racist and xenophobic rhetoric.

Interestingly, Ott was himself the child of immigrants. Charles was the third of five children born to Protestant immigrants from Switzerland.[7] In the Klan's political calculus, Protestant immigrants from western and central Europe were preferable to Catholic and Jewish immigrants from southern and eastern Europe.[8]

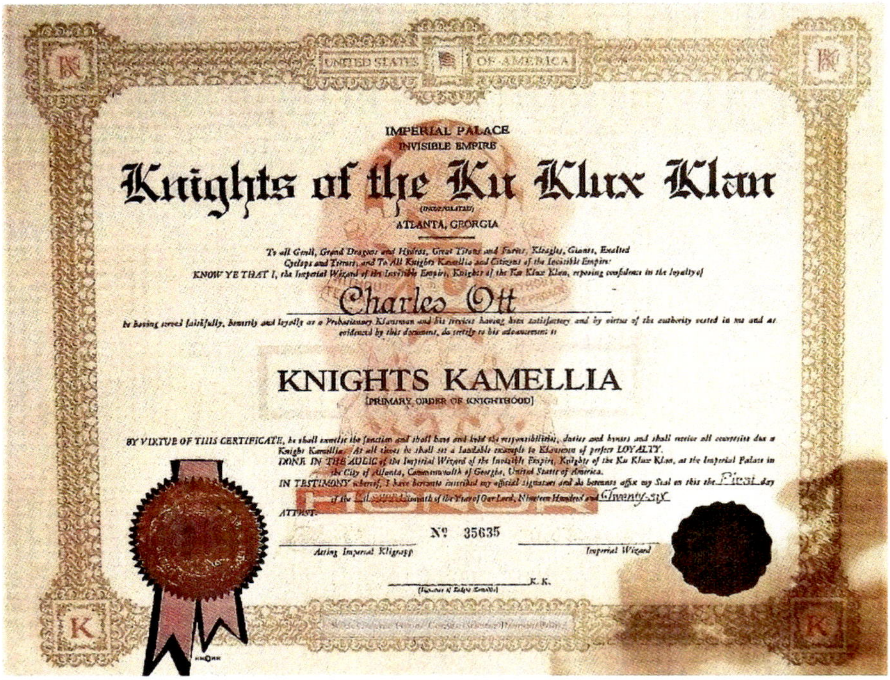

Ku Klux Klan certificate for Charles Ott, promoting him from probationary to full membership (1926). *From Ku Klux Klan File, East Rochester Department of Local History.*

Following his parents' deaths, Charles and his sister Ada lived on the family farm, growing wheat and apples.[9] He later ran a trucking company.[10]

Despite the recruiting rallies in Rochester, the group never caught on in the city. According to former city historian Blake McKelvey, there was little resentment upon which the Klan could build. Relatively few African Americans resided in the city in the 1920s, and relations between Jews, Catholics, and Protestants were amicable. But the surrounding towns and rural areas saw Klan activity.[11]

In the fall of 1923, Klan activities were reported in Henrietta and Hemlock.[12] There are also records of KKK activities in Albion,[13] Fairport,[14] Brockport, Honeoye Falls, Pittsford,[15] Spencerport,[16] and other nearby communities.

The largest local Klan rally was held Saturday and Sunday, September 25–26, 1926, in East Rochester. Klansmen and women from ten counties flocked in full regalia to the farm of Charles Ott at Washington and Ivy streets. The thirty-six acres held by the family provided a useful venue for the regional gathering. Exactly how many attended is a matter of dispute. Estimates run the gamut from 1,000 to 19,000, but no official total was ever released.

Newspaper coverage of the gathering was extensive, so we have a good idea of the activities. Fifty tents were set up, blazing with lights strung for the event. Among the most brilliant were the lights illuminating the tents of Klan officials, including that of women Ku Klux Klan officers in their red and white gowns and capes.[17]

Between the American and Christian flags was an electrically powered burning cross. On the front of the platform was a banner bearing the words: "One Flag, Old Glory; One Language, American [sic]; One School, Public" (the slogan indicating opposition to Gov. Smith's proposal for state support for parochial schools). Local and Klan officials delivered speeches throughout each day. Saturday evening, Klan initiation ceremonies were conducted, during which three fiery crosses were burned, including one fifty feet tall. The final event was the Sunday morning parade. Beginning at daylight, the Klan filled Commercial Street from side to side, marched down the thoroughfare, and turned right onto Washington Street, stopping at the Ott farm, where they dispersed.[18]

Thousands gathered to view the public proceedings the first night of the gathering. There were fears brawls might break out during the gathering; however, none occurred. A close call arose the following day, when a local journalist and photographer were denied permission to cover the event because the latter was Catholic. Words were exchanged, but the professionals left after being denied entry.[19]

The 1926 gathering was the high point of Klan activity locally. The reasons for the decline are many—from the high cost of membership[20] and a New York State law requiring organizations to report the names of all members[21] to local resistance to Klan activities.[22] Another contributing factor was the failure of Alfred Smith's campaign for president in 1928. Smith, New York's Democrat governor, lost to Republican Herbert Hoover, a former secretary of commerce. The Hoover camp launched one of the most virulently anti-Catholic campaigns in American history, freely drawing on the stereotype of a Catholic president taking orders from the Pope. With Smith's resounding defeat in an electoral college landslide, political power was seen as securely held in the hands of what the Klan called "100% Americans." Ironically, with victory secured, Klan membership was no longer thought necessary to protect so-called "real American interests."[23] ■

1. *Constitution and Laws of the Knights of the Ku Klux Klan Incorporated* (Atlanta: Knights of the Ku Klux Klan, 1921), 109.
2. "Official Document No. 405," in *Important Imperial Edicts and Documents* (Atlanta: Ku Klux Klan, 1930), 9.
3. Linda Gordon, *The Second Coming of the KKK: The Ku Klux Klan of the 1920s and the American Political Tradition* (New York: W. W. Norton and Co., 2017), 12.
4. "Klan Meeting Rumored Thursday: Place Secret," *Democrat & Chronicle*, December 12, 1922, 1, 22.
5. "I. R. Hignett, Grand Organizer of Atlanta, Harangues Audience in Hickatoo Hall for Over Two Hours," Rochester *Times-Union*, November 23, 1923, 1.
6. Rory McVeigh, *The Rise of the Ku Klux Klan: Right-Wing Movements and National Politics* 32 (Minneapolis: University of Minnesota Press, 2009), 184–85.
7. 1880 US Census Bureau, Pittsford, Monroe County, New York, population schedule, enumeration district 62, p. 21 (written), dwelling 204, family 205, Charles Ott in household of Samuel Ott.
8. McVeigh, *Rise of the Ku Klux Klan*, 66–67.
9. James Burlingame (East Rochester Village Historian), in discussion with author, May 10, 2019.

10. "C. W. Ott Succumbs," *Democrat & Chronicle,* June 17, 1963, D6.
11. Blake McKelvey, *Rochester, the Quest for Quality, 1890–1925* (Cambridge, MA: Harvard University Press, 1956), 366–67.
12. "Ku Klux Meeting," *The Catholic Journal,* November 30, 1923, 5. The last paragraph recounts burning crosses in the towns.
13. Albion hosted Region 8's Klonvocation in 1925. See the photograph "Klan Meeting" in Avis A. Townsend, *Albion* (Charleston, SC: Arcadia Publishing Co., 2005), 19.
14. "The Local News in Fairport and Vicinity," *Monroe County Mail,* November 22, 1923, 2. The article recounts a cross burning on John Bunyan's farm (Fairport and Jefferson Roads). Several months earlier, two Klan representatives tried to recruit new members among "well known citizens" but without success.
15. Arch Merrill, "Venomous Black Book Tells: When Men Hid Faces Behind Masks of KKK," *Democrat & Chronicle,* May 31, 1953, C2.
16. "Empire State News in Brief," *Perry Record,* January 10, 1924, 3. A news item in the column indicates the local KKK branch in Spencerport had eighty members.
17. "Fiery Cross Burned Between Flags on Platform," *Democrat & Chronicle,* September 26, 1926, 25.
18. "Fiery Cross Burned," *Democrat & Chronicle,* September 26, 1926.
19. "Reporter Barred at Gathering of Klan Because Accompanied by Catholic Photographer," *Democrat & Chronicle,* September 26, 1926, 25.
20. Gordon, *Second Coming,* 66. According to Gordon, membership was costly. Members had to pay to join as well as pay for initiation, annual dues, and the cost of the costume (which was so designed that it could not be made at home). In addition, members were dunned for insurance, political contributions, gifts to churches, and special projects.
21. *Laws of the State of New York Passed at the One Hundred and Forty-Sixth Session of the Legislature* . . . [etc.] (Albany, NY: J. B. Lyons Co., 1923), 1110.
22. Numerous sources testify to local opposition to Klan activities. See, for example, "Post Would Dismiss from Legion Any Who Enter Ku Klux Klan," *Democrat & Chronicle,* December 15, 1922, 39; "Dansville Men Watchful While K.K.K. Meets," Rochester *Times-Union,* November 24, 1923, 3; "Grangers Hand K.O. to KKK," *The Brockport Republic,* December 20, 1923, 10.
23. McVeigh, *Rise of the Ku Klux Klan,* 195.